Teen Trials
JOURNAL

TURNING TRIALS INTO TRIUMPHS

Kim Leane

good seed press

Teen Trials Journal: Turning Trials into Triumphs
by Kim Leane

Copyright © 2019 by Kim Leane
All rights reserved.

Good Seed Press titles may be purchased in bulk for educational, business, fundraising, or sales promotional use. For information please contact Good Seed Press via email at contact@kimleane.com.

All rights reserved. Except in the case of brief quotations embodied in critical articles and reviews, no portion of this book may be reproduced, stored in a retrieval system, or transmitted in any form or by any means – electronic, mechanical, photocopy, recording, scanning, or other – without the prior written permission from the author.

Unless otherwise indicated, all Scripture quotations are taken from the Holy Bible, New International Version®, NIV® Copyright © 1973, 1978, 1984, 2011 by Biblica, Inc.® Used by permission. All rights reserved worldwide.

Scripture quotations marked NLT are taken from the Holy Bible, New Living Translation, copyright © 1996, 2004, 2015 by Tyndale House Foundation. Used by permission of Tyndale House Publishers, Inc., Carol Stream, Illinois 60188. All rights reserved.

Printed in the United States of America
ISBN: 978-1-7342061-0-4

I'd love to hear how you are using your journal! Tag me in a post and connect with me here:

- ★ *Instagram*: @kimleaneauthor
- ★ *Facebook*: @kimleaneauthor
- ★ *Website*: www.kimleane.com
- ★ *Email*: contact@kimleane.com

Table of Contents

Introduction 2
How to Use this Journal 4

Trial Topics:
    Addiction 6
    Anxiety and Depression 10
    Dating Dilemmas 14
    Failures 18
    Friendship Frustrations 22
    Health Concerns 26
    Loneliness 30
    Loss and Grief 34
    Mean Messages 38
    Money Matters 42
    Problems with Parents 46
    Rejection 50
    Responsibilities 54
    Sibling Strife 58
    Sleep Deprived 62
    Temptation 66
    Uncontrollable Circumstances 70
    Unknown Future 74

Blank Journal Pages 78
Answered Prayers 82
Draw it Out 84
Additional Scriptures 86

Introduction

So, you've discovered that being a teenager has its bad days. This is one of the universal truths of humankind. Adolescent trials come without discrimination to the rich and poor, extrovert and introvert, athlete and mathlete... no matter what country you live in, all of us struggle in some way through these challenging years.

One thing I want you to know is that God is with you every step of the way through this season in life, and He loves you the same as He always has! But that is easy to forget if you become overwhelmed by the many trials you encounter. Sometimes you just can't seem to get a break! *This journal is designed to help you see exactly how God is ready and able to help you through them, so that you can have victory and an incredible testimony of how God turned your trials into triumphs!*

As you persevere through your trials, keep these four truths in mind:

1. God knows what you're going through

- Jesus experienced ALL the trials you do: rejection, loss, disappointment, temptation, parents who weren't ready for him to grow up – you name it, He lived it.
- God loves you like no one on earth ever can. No one.
- The Bible promises you will have trials (John 16:33), and your perseverance through them will help your faith mature (James 1:2-4). But God doesn't want you to go through them without His help (Psalm 46:1) – He is with you in the middle of them just as he was for Shadrach, Meshach and Abednego (Daniel 3).

2. God wants to talk to you

- The Holy Spirit is the helper He's given to all who are His children. The Spirit is in you (1 Corinthians 6:19), speaks only what God says (John 16:13), and helps you when you don't know how to pray (Romans 8:26). How awesome is that!
- You need to learn how to hear God's "voice." You do this by:
  - <u>Talking to God about everything.</u> He knows it already, but it's like a friendship... He wants you to include Him in the discussion.
  - <u>Reading your Bible regularly.</u> The Bible is God talking to you. You know your parent's voice because you've heard it for years. Reading God's word is your primary way of hearing God, and then you'll begin to see how He speaks in other ways. A good place to start is in any of the New Testament gospels (Matthew, Mark, Luke or John), to read how Jesus lived and what His mission on earth was.

- <u>Writing in a journal.</u> This will help you clarify your thoughts and feelings, and will be a place to write what He shows you in His Word and in your spirit. If you want, you can choose a different journal for your everyday discussions with God and what He is showing you. In this journal, you can focus on the trials you are experiencing, and the outcomes will be the evidence of how God is protecting you and providing solutions for you in your specific circumstances.

3. God wants to direct you

- ★ The Holy Spirit acts as your guide (John 16:13).
- ★ He has plans to give you an abundant life and keep you from harm (Jeremiah 29:11).
- ★ He has "good works" prepared in advance for you to do (Ephesians 2:10) and will direct your path to accomplish them (Proverbs 16:9).

4. God expects you to turn your faith into action

- ★ This is your response. Wherever He leads you, be willing to follow (John 10:2-4). Like a sheep who trusts its shepherd. "Following" God doesn't just mean believing in Him, it means *obeying* Him.
- ★ God rarely shows you steps A to Z up front. Start with step A by doing it *in faith*, believing God will show you step B at just the right time. The Bible is full of examples of people (teenagers even!) having to do something in faith before God provided the answer or victory.
- ★ If you aren't sure how God is leading you, ponder in your heart what you want to do, check your motives, see if your gut feeling/instinct is in line with God's word, and then take that first step (make a decision) and ask God to confirm or correct the course you are on.
- ★ God will bless your steps in faith – He always wants to encourage you when you are doing His will! Ask Him to give you a sign. Ask for wisdom and understanding and patience to endure through the trial. The obstacles may still be there for you to push through. But in the midst of them you can watch Him show up and show off His great power in your life!

I hope that in recording the details of the personal trials you are experiencing, putting your faith into action by taking a step forward, and documenting how God helped you overcome them, you will be blessed with an amazing written testimony of God working ALL things out for your good (Romans 8:28)!

How to use this journal

There are 18 different topics in this journal that are common to teenagers. Unlike a blank journal, where you might write down all your thoughts, feelings or prayers, this journal gives you specific guidance to work through a variety of hardships in your life.

When you are encountering a trial, find the corresponding four-page journal layout that covers that topic and work through each section. It's okay if it takes a long time for the trial to be resolved. God may be allowing it so He can strengthen your character, even if this issue doesn't seem to be resolving. Either way God has blessings for you, and He will see you through to the end (Philippians 1:6)!

Each topic's journal pages have these sections:

1. **My dilemma** – write the date and the details of the trial you are facing.

2. **Ideal outcome** – imagine how it would look if it were resolved in an ideal way (this would look like a 'win-win' for all parties, relationships are strengthened not broken, justice is served, healing is complete, etc.). The point of this step is to visualize a positive outcome, and to entrust that outcome to the God who actually can and does perform miracles. He actually wants to do way more than you can even imagine (Ephesians 3:20)! If you believe He will answer your prayer, then it will come to pass in the way that He wants it to (Matthew 21:22).

3. **God's truth** – look up the Bible verses and write down the main idea or what stands out. These include instructions, encouragement, examples and God's promises. Verses are taken from the NIV unless noted with "NLT." Use a Bible app to look up the translation if you don't already have that Bible. Then also write out how the verses apply to your situation.

4. **My convictions** – after you read the verses, pray and ask God to show you if your motives aren't right or if you are contributing to the problem (Psalm 139:23-24); write these out and be humble and honest with yourself and God. He will honor that! It can be tempting to only blame other people or the circumstances surrounding your situation, but try to identify how you could make a change – in perspective, attitude, or behavior. The Holy Spirit is quite good at convicting us! This is the starting point for the change you are looking for.

5. **My decisions** – when you are ready to address your struggle, this is where you can write out your dialogue with God and the steps you begin to take. There are also some guiding questions to help you process your situation. Think through scenarios of how other people involved might respond to your planned actions, so you can be prepared. (Asking your parent's help in brainstorming steps and probable responses would be an excellent idea here). Talk to God about what you should do. After you decide on and carry out an action step, write down what happened, how it made you feel, and especially how God gave you courage or

new insight. Repeat for as many action steps as it takes. This process could take days or weeks or even months, so don't feel rushed.

6. **Final outcome** – if you think your trial has come to an end, write down the date and how it ended. Think about how God guided you to it. You can write a prayer of praise to Him because ultimately this is about seeing Him actively working in your life and deepening your relationship with Him! If you don't see the result you hoped for or it seems that no resolution came, keep in mind that God's faithfulness doesn't change. Growing spiritually is a valuable outcome from any trial, and God may be considering that to be your victory.

7. **You're in Good Company** – did you know that there are examples in the Bible of someone like you who has endured similar trials? Read about them to be encouraged!

Your journey is unique because God created you that way. **Your purpose in life** is to be in a growing relationship with God, do His will, and bring Him glory. This never changes! Jesus is a real friend, and He is your constant help in times of trouble. I hope this journal is your proof that He is always there for you.

I also encourage you to seek help from your parents, pastor, coach, teacher, or a trusted friend, especially if you reach a point where you don't think a resolution is possible. This can be a discouraging position to be in, even more so if you feel alone. It might seem like every other teenager has their act together, but trust me, they don't. They are struggling too. No one wants you to suffer through a trial, and many people are nearby who are trustworthy and can provide you with the support you need. None of us can do life alone, particularly when we are going through a hard time.

Lastly, in addition to the Bible verses I've included in each topic, try reading through the Psalms, one chapter per day. You will be amazed at how many times the writer (mostly King David) was in trouble and needed God to rescue him. He didn't hold back letting God know how he was feeling, even expressing his fear, anger and desperation. You should try that sometime – God can definitely handle it!

> **The righteous cry out, and the Lord hears them;**
> **he delivers them from all their troubles.**
> ~ Psalm 34:17

I pray that this journal is an anchor during tough times and that victory will be yours in the power of Jesus' name!

Addiction

Addiction is s serious beast. It touches on spiritual concepts like idolatry, slavery, and self-control. But it is not limited to the common problems of alcohol, smoking or viewing illicit images. Think about how much time you spend doing (or desiring) activities that keep you from having a healthy balance in life. Do you obsess about social media, video games, food or shopping? Do you rely on substances like caffeine or pain medicine? It's possible to even turn a healthy activity into an obsession that you then depend on in unhealthy ways. God wants for you to be self-controlled. Addiction has a gripping mind-body connection that leaves you feeling out of control. It is rarely overcome alone, so please ask for help from your family, doctor or pastor. When you see the signs of addiction as a full-scale attack that Satan is carrying out (Ephesians 6:12), you can start fighting back with spiritual truth and Holy Spirit power and stop it from taking over.

My dilemma

_____
_____
_____

Ideal outcome

_____
_____
_____

God's truth

Provers 25:28 _____
Psalm 32:3-5 _____
1 Corinthians 6:12 _____
Romans 8:5 _____
Romans 6:12-14, 21-22 _____
Ephesians 5:18 _____
1 Peter 5:8-9 _____
1 Thessalonians 4:3-4 _____
1 Corinthians 10:13 _____
Titus 2:3,6,11-12 _____
Galatians 5:16-24 _____
2 Corinthians 7:9-10 _____

How these truths apply to my situation

_____
_____
_____
_____
_____

My convictions

_____
_____
_____
_____

My decisions

What am I feeling right now?
_____
_____

What worse outcomes might happen if I don't resolve this?
_____
_____
_____

If I can't resolve it myself and it feels like I just have to cope, what is my prayer right now?
_____
_____
_____

What would it take to achieve my ideal outcome? Who can I ask to help me accomplish this?
_____
_____
_____
_____
_____

Addiction

My decisions (continued)

Talk to God about it; write out what you want to do, what you are saying to God, what He is saying to you, and what events are unfolding, as you work at achieving your ideal outcome.

_____
_____
_____
_____
_____
_____
_____
_____
_____
_____
_____
_____

Final outcome

_____
_____
_____
_____
_____
_____
_____
_____

You're in good company

Israelites (Idolatry) – read Ezekiel 14:1-8

Solomon – read 1 Kings 3:1, 11:1-6

Early believers – read Galatians 4:8-11 and 5:13,16-21

May God himself, the God of peace, sanctify you through and through. May your whole spirit, soul and body be kept blameless at the coming of our Lord Jesus Christ.
– 1 Thessalonians 5:23

Anxiety and Depression

Sometimes you can become so worried or reach deeper lows and not bounce back. When sadness, stress, sickness or pressures of the teenage life keep weighing on your mind, depression and anxiety are very real and can be very scary. You can feel like you are in a pit of despair. Please make sure your family, doctor or pastor know how you are struggling. Do not go through this alone! Stay connected to your tribe of family, friends, and church because you will find strength in belonging. No matter what the causes are of your mental trials, always take it to God. Prayer will be your strongest spiritual weapon. With help from God, family and medical professionals, you can overcome this!

My dilemma

_____
_____
_____
_____
_____

Ideal outcome

_____
_____
_____

God's truth

Proverbs 12:25 _____
Psalm 69:1-3,14-15 (NLT) _____
Psalm 94:17-19 _____
Lamentations 3:19-26 _____
1 Peter 5:7 _____
John 14:27 _____
Romans 12:2 _____

How these truths apply to my situation

_____
_____
_____

My convictions

_____
_____
_____
_____

My decisions

What am I feeling right now?
_____
_____

What's the worst thing that could happen if I tried to resolve this? Or if I don't?
_____
_____
_____

If I can't resolve it and it feels like I just have to cope, what is my prayer right now?
_____
_____
_____

What are the lies that the devil is trying to make me believe?
_____
_____
_____

What could be some positive things that can come from this struggle?
_____
_____
_____

What would it take to achieve my ideal outcome?
_____
_____
_____
_____

Anxiety and Depression

My decisions (continued)

Talk to God about it; write out what you want to do, what you are saying to God, what He is saying to you, and what events are unfolding, as you work at achieving your ideal outcome.

_____
_____
_____
_____
_____
_____
_____
_____

Final outcome

_____
_____
_____
_____
_____
_____

You're in good company

Job – read Job 2 and 3 and 7:16 and 10:20

David – read 1 Samuel 30:3-6 and Psalm 102

Elijah – read 1 Kings 19:1-5

You will keep in perfect peace those whose minds are steadfast, because they trust in you.
– Isaiah 26:3

Dating Dilemmas

Oh the excitement that comes from having a new crush! Next thing you know, you are dating. You are in uncharted territory. Dating can be fun, and it feels good to be special to someone. Often these relationships don't last long, but that doesn't mean they have to end poorly. How you treat your "significant other" and the boundaries you set will have a big effect on how well you survive it.

My dilemma

_____
_____
_____
_____
_____
_____

Ideal outcome

_____
_____
_____
_____

God's truth

Jeremiah 17:9 _____
2 Corinthians 6:14 _____
1 Corinthians 13:4-8 _____
1 Samuel 16:7 _____
Proverbs 12:26 _____
Luke 6:31 _____

How these truths apply to my situation

_____
_____
_____
_____
_____
_____

My convictions

_____
_____
_____
_____

My decisions

What am I feeling right now?
_____
_____

What's the worst thing that could happen if I tried to resolve this? Or if I don't?
_____
_____
_____

If I can't resolve it and it feels like I just have to cope, what is my prayer right now?
_____
_____
_____

Is a positive outcome most likely found in getting out of the situation or persevering through it? Why?
_____
_____
_____

How can I grow as a person from this struggle?
_____
_____
_____

What would it take to achieve my ideal outcome?
_____
_____
_____
_____

Dating Dilemmas

My decisions (continued)

Talk to God about it; write out what you want to do, what you are saying to God, what He is saying to you, and what events are unfolding, as you work at achieving your ideal outcome.

_____

Final outcome

_____

You're in good company

Jacob – read Genesis 29:15-30

Samson – read Judges 13-17

Samaritan woman – read John 4:15-19

Do not arouse or awaken love until it so desires.
– Song of Songs 2:7b

Failures

Let's be clear: <u>you</u> are not a failure. You have inherent, priceless value and immense potential. You are a child of the King! When you "fail" it usually means you didn't meet your expectations. It's actually a valuable learning experience, even though it doesn't feel like it at the time. "Success is stumbling from failure to failure with no loss of enthusiasm." ~Winston Churchill. Failure is so inescapable that it will happen continually in life. You won't always pass the test, make the team, earn the high grade, win the scholarship, or get the job. You'll also make mistakes. Be the kind of person who is resilient, who still dreams big and puts yourself out there to try for what you really want – even when it's a long shot.

My dilemma

_____
_____
_____
_____

Ideal outcome

_____
_____
_____
_____

God's truth

2 Corinthians 4:7-10 _____
Proverbs 15:22 _____
2 Corinthians 12:9-10 _____
James 1:2-4 _____
Isaiah 40:29-31 _____

How these truths apply to my situation

_____
_____
_____
_____

My convictions

_____
_____
_____
_____

My decisions

What am I feeling right now?
_____
_____

If I can't resolve it and it feels like I just have to cope, what is my prayer right now?
_____
_____
_____

Is a positive outcome most likely found in getting out of the situation or persevering through it? Why?
_____
_____
_____

What could be some positive things that can come from this struggle?
_____
_____
_____

What are the lies that the devil is trying to make me believe?
_____
_____
_____

What would it take to achieve my ideal outcome?
_____
_____
_____
_____

Failures

My decisions (continued)

Talk to God about it; write out what you want to do, what you are saying to God, what He is saying to you, and what events are unfolding, as you work at achieving your ideal outcome.

_____
_____
_____
_____
_____
_____
_____
_____
_____
_____

Final outcome

_____
_____
_____
_____
_____
_____
_____
_____

You're in good company

Jonah – read Jonah 1:1-17

Israelites – read Joshua 7:2-8 and 1 Samuel 4:10-11

Peter – read Luke 22:31-34, 54-62

Disciples – read Matthew 17:15-20

And we know that in all things God works for the good of those who love him, who have been called according to his purpose.

– Romans 8:28

Friendship Frustrations

You may be having trouble with a friend, but keep this in mind: all teenagers are changing and trying to figure out who they are. They often make poor choices too. Your hopes for how this friendship turns out will affect your decisions on how to proceed. Learning to work through disagreements and misunderstandings is important, but sometimes the path you are on may not be the same one that your friend is on, and that's okay. Some friendships are not forever.

My dilemma

_____
_____
_____
_____

Ideal outcome

_____
_____
_____
_____

God's truth

Proverbs 12:26 _____
Job 6:14-15 _____
1 Corinthians 15:33 _____
Proverbs 16:28 _____
Proverbs 22:24-25 _____
Proverbs 17:17 _____
Colossians 3:12-14 _____

How these truths apply to my situation

_____
_____
_____
_____

My convictions

_____
_____
_____
_____

My decisions

What am I feeling right now?
_____
_____

What's the worst thing that could happen if I tried to resolve this? Or if I don't?
_____
_____
_____

If I can't resolve it and it feels like I just have to cope, what is my prayer right now?
_____
_____
_____

Is a positive outcome most likely found in getting out of the situation or persevering through it? Why?
_____
_____
_____

How can I grow as a person from this struggle?
_____
_____
_____

What would it take to achieve my ideal outcome?
_____
_____
_____
_____

Friendship Frustrations

My decisions (continued)

Talk to God about it; write out what you want to do, what you are saying to God, what He is saying to you, and what events are unfolding, as you work at achieving your ideal outcome.

Final outcome

You're in good company

Jesus & Peter – read Matthew 26:31-35, 56b-58, 69-75

Apostles – read Acts 15:36-40

Disciples – read Luke 22:24-30 and John 21:20-24

There is no greater love than to lay down one's life for one's friends.
– John 15:13 (NLT)

Health Concerns

We may never know why some people seem perfectly healthy while others have physical ailments that are painful or long-lasting. If you're suffering you might question God's goodness, especially if it is something linked to your God-given DNA. You may see your acne or deformity or cancer as a trial you don't deserve, and you are right. But God doesn't judge your outward appearance, and He works out your sickness for your benefit. Healing is definitely part of God's plan for you, in His perfect timing.

My dilemma

_____
_____
_____
_____

Ideal outcome

_____
_____
_____
_____

God's truth

Psalm 119:107 _____
Job 36:15 _____
Psalm 73:26 _____
2 Corinthians 4:16-18 _____
1 Samuel 16:7 _____
Isaiah 38:16-17 _____

How these truths apply to my situation

_____
_____
_____
_____
_____

My convictions

_____
_____
_____
_____

My decisions

What am I feeling right now?
_____
_____

What's the worst thing that could happen if I tried to resolve this? Or if I don't?
_____
_____
_____

If I can't resolve it and it feels like I just have to cope, what is my prayer right now?
_____
_____
_____

What are the lies that the devil is trying to make me believe?
_____
_____
_____

What could be some positive things that can come from this struggle?
_____
_____
_____

What would it take to achieve my ideal outcome?
_____
_____
_____
_____

My decisions (continued)

Talk to God about it; write out what you want to do, what you are saying to God, what He is saying to you, and what events are unfolding, as you work at achieving your ideal outcome.

Final outcome

You're in good company

Jesus — read Isaiah 53:4-5 and Hebrews 5:7

Paralytic — read John 5:2-9

Paul — read 2 Corinthians 12:7-10

He will wipe every tear from their eyes. There will be no more death or mourning or crying or pain, for the old order of things has passed away.

– Revelation 21:4

loneliness

You may be surrounded by a sea of people, yet you feel so alone. You are loved by many, but you feel like you are not truly known. Every person experiences this dreadful sense of loneliness at various times. If you are experiencing this now, start by asking God to help you find a true friend with whom you can be yourself. Jesus is already that, but you need the human kind as well. Remember God will use this experience to draw you closer to Him, and He will provide for your needs.

My dilemma

_____
_____
_____
_____
_____
_____

Ideal outcome

_____
_____
_____
_____
_____

God's truth

Psalm 25:16-17 _____
Psalm 88:18 _____
Genesis 2:18 _____
Ecclesiastes 4:9-10 _____
Psalm 34:18 _____

How these truths apply to my situation

_____
_____
_____
_____
_____

My convictions

_____
_____
_____
_____

My decisions

What am I feeling right now?
_____
_____

Which individuals am I truly authentic with (in person, on social media, etc.)?
_____
_____
_____

If it feels like I am just coping, what is my prayer right now?
_____
_____
_____

Am I hanging around people who are a lot like me, or very different? Do I like the differences? Are they people who fill me up or drain my energy?
_____
_____
_____
_____

What could be some positive things that can come from this struggle?
_____
_____
_____

What would it take to achieve my ideal outcome?
_____
_____
_____
_____

Loneliness

My decisions (continued)

Talk to God about it; write out what you want to do, what you are saying to God, what He is saying to you, and what events are unfolding, as you work at achieving your ideal outcome.

Final outcome

_____

You're in good company

Jesus – read Luke 5:16 and John 16:32 and Mark 14:50-54

David – read Psalm 25:16-22

God sets the lonely in families...
– Psalm 68:6

Loss and Grief

If there is anything that can be utterly devastating, it is losing someone or something that was so important to you. Your grief is real and raw and you don't know how you will recover. This will definitely take time, so be patient with yourself. God grieves with you and wants to restore your joy. He uses all these hard experiences to draw you closer to Him and will use them in your life for your good. It will just take time to see the whole story unfold.

My dilemma

_____
_____
_____
_____

Ideal outcome

_____
_____
_____
_____

God's truth

2 Corinthians 1:3-4 _____
Matthew 5:3-4 _____
Psalm 126:5-6 _____
Jeremiah 31:13 _____
Isaiah 61:1-3 _____
Revelation 21:4 _____

How these truths apply to my situation

_____
_____
_____
_____
_____

My convictions

_____
_____
_____
_____

My decisions

What am I feeling right now?
_____
_____

What's the worst thing that could happen if I tried to resolve this? Or if I don't?
_____
_____
_____

If I can't resolve it and it feels like I just have to cope, what is my prayer right now?
_____
_____
_____

What are some things in my life that bring me joy?
_____
_____
_____

What could be some positive things that can come from this struggle?
_____
_____
_____

What would it take to achieve my ideal outcome?
_____
_____
_____
_____

Loss and Grief

My decisions (continued)
Talk to God about it; write out what you want to do, what you are saying to God, what He is saying to you, and what events are unfolding, as you work at achieving your ideal outcome.

Final outcome

_____

You're in good company

Jesus – read Matthew 14:6-13a and John 11:1-3,14-36

Job – read Job 1 and 2; 42:10-17 and James 5:10-11

Mary & Martha – read John 11:1-37

Naomi – read Ruth 1:1-21; 4:3-22

The Lord is close to the brokenhearted and saves those who are crushed in spirit.

— Psalm 34:18

Mean Messages

Gossipy girls, trash-talking teammates, and bullies who enjoy making your life miserable. You are so sick of them! Thinking about having to face them again can suck the joy right out of you. It can also be scary to stand up for the values and beliefs you live by, when some of your peers may mock you. These are tricky situations because their behaviors reveal a sadness within them that you can't fix. Prayer, confidence in who you are, and kindness will be your best defense – and offense.

My dilemma

_____
_____
_____
_____

Ideal outcome

_____
_____
_____
_____

God's truth

Psalm 109:1-5 _____
Psalm 73 _____
Romans 12:17-19 _____
Psalm 27:1-3 _____
2 Thessalonians 1:6-7 _____
Matthew 5:11-12 _____

How these truths apply to my situation

_____
_____
_____
_____
_____

My convictions

_____
_____
_____
_____

My decisions

What am I feeling right now?
_____
_____

What's the worst thing that could happen if I tried to resolve this? Or if I don't?
_____
_____
_____

If I can't resolve it and it feels like I just have to cope, what is my prayer right now?
_____
_____
_____

Is a positive outcome most likely found in getting out of the situation or persevering through it? Why?
_____
_____
_____
_____

How can I grow as a person from this struggle?
_____
_____
_____

What would it take to achieve my ideal outcome?
_____
_____
_____
_____

My decisions (continued)

Talk to God about it; write out what you want to do, what you are saying to God, what He is saying to you, and what events are unfolding, as you work at achieving your ideal outcome.

_____
_____
_____
_____
_____
_____
_____
_____
_____
_____

Final outcome

_____
_____
_____
_____
_____
_____
_____

You're in good company

Jesus – read Matthew 2:13; 12:14; 26:1-4,67-68; 27:1-2,26-31,39-44 and John 5:16-18 and Hebrews 12:3

Hannah – read 1 Samuel 1:1-17,19-20

Paul & Silas – read Acts 16:19-24

Hatred stirs up conflict, but love covers over all wrongs.
– Proverbs 10:12

Money Matters

The pitfalls with money often fall into one of two categories: there's rarely enough, or you mismanage what you have. These extremes can leave you feeling frustrated and anxious. Money issues can also reveal a lack of contentment or a lack of self-control. God wants to help you get a handle on that!

My dilemma

_____
_____
_____
_____

Ideal outcome

_____
_____
_____
_____

God's truth

Lack of money:
1 Samuel 2:7-8 _____
Proverbs 10:4 _____
Proverbs 15:16 _____
Mark 12:41-44 _____
Proverbs 23:4-5 _____

Wealth and wisdom:
Psalm 49:16-20 _____
Proverbs 3:9-10 _____
Ecclesiastes 5:10-14 _____
Matthew 19:16-30 _____
Luke 16:10-13 _____
1 Timothy 6:17-19 _____

How these truths apply to my situation

_____
_____
_____
_____

My convictions

_____
_____
_____
_____

My decisions

What am I feeling right now?
_____
_____

Who in my life displays good attitudes about money or good money management habits?
_____
_____
_____

If I can't resolve it and it feels like I just have to cope, what is my prayer right now?
_____
_____
_____

What could be some positive things that can come from this struggle?
_____
_____
_____

What would it take to achieve my ideal outcome?
_____
_____
_____

My decisions (continued)

Talk to God about it; write out what you want to do, what you are saying to God, what He is saying to you, and what events are unfolding, as you work at achieving your ideal outcome.

_____
_____
_____
_____
_____
_____
_____
_____
_____

Final outcome

_____
_____
_____
_____
_____
_____

You're in good company

Widow with oil – read 2 Kings 4:1-7

Poor widow – read Luke 21:1-4

Prodigal Son – read Luke 15:11-32

Seek the Kingdom of God above all else, and live righteously, and he will give you everything you need.

– Matthew 6:33 (NLT)

Problems with Parents

You're not a kid anymore, and with age comes some new expectations. Your parents may need you to contribute more around the house, or they have become stricter with their rules. They might also see your great potential and challenge you to do better or more. Sometimes even their good intentions, while motivated by love, can feel like a burden to you. Or worse, maybe your own parents are unkind to you or each other. God definitely has some instructions on how you will be victorious in this trial.

My dilemma

_____
_____
_____
_____
_____

Ideal outcome

_____
_____
_____
_____
_____

God's truth

Proverbs 6:20-22 _____
Proverbs 15:5 _____
Colossians 3:20 _____
Exodus 20:12 _____
Ephesians 6:1-3 _____
Romans 1:29-32 _____

How these truths apply to my situation

_____
_____
_____
_____
_____

My convictions

_____
_____
_____
_____

My decisions

What am I feeling right now?
_____
_____

What's the worst thing that could happen if I tried to resolve this? Or if I don't?
_____
_____
_____

If I can't resolve it and it feels like I just have to cope, what is my prayer right now?
_____
_____
_____

What responses to my parents would be most respectful, even if they seem hard to do?
_____
_____
_____

What could be some positive things that can come from this struggle?
_____
_____
_____

What would it take to achieve my ideal outcome?
_____
_____
_____
_____

Problems with Parents

My decisions (continued)

Talk to God about it; write out what you want to do, what you are saying to God, what He is saying to you, and what events are unfolding, as you work at achieving your ideal outcome.

Final outcome

You're in good company

Jesus – read Luke 2:41-52 and John 2:1-5

Esau – read Genesis 27:1-40

Jonathon – read 1 Samuel 20:27-34

Absalom (King David's son) – read 2 Samuel 13:28-33; 14:23-24,28; 15:1-17,37; 16:5-11; 17:1-4; 18:6-15

Listen to advice and accept discipline, and at the end you will be counted among the wise.
– Proverbs 19:20

Rejection

Nothing stings like rejection. Maybe you didn't get into the school club you wanted or college you worked so hard for. Maybe you have a friend who ditched you without saying a word, or you got cut from the team. You can be left feeling hurt, embarrassed and seriously disappointed! Like failures, rejection is a trial you will encounter all throughout life. Practicing healthy responses now will help you in so many ways in the future.

My dilemma

Ideal outcome

God's truth

Luke 21:16
1 Peter 2:4
Isaiah 41:9
Isaiah 53:3
Psalm 94:14
Psalm 102:17

How these truths apply to my situation

My convictions

_____
_____
_____
_____

My decisions

What am I feeling right now?
_____
_____

What's the worst thing that could happen if I tried to resolve this? Or if I don't?
_____
_____
_____

If I can't resolve it and it feels like I just have to cope, what is my prayer right now?
_____
_____
_____

Is a positive outcome most likely found in getting out of the situation or persevering through it? Why?
_____
_____
_____
_____

How can I grow as a person from this struggle?
_____
_____

What would it take to achieve my ideal outcome?
_____
_____
_____
_____

My decisions (continued)

Talk to God about it; write out what you want to do, what you are saying to God, what He is saying to you, and what events are unfolding, as you work at achieving your ideal outcome.

Final outcome

You're in good company

Jesus – read Luke 17:25 and Matthew 13:53-57; 17:22-23; 26:47-55,69-75 and John 6:60-66 and Isaiah 53:3

David – read Psalm 41:9 and 109:1-5

Moses – read Exodus 2:11-15 and Acts 7:22-39

Everyone will hate you because of me,
but the one who stands firm to the end will be saved.

– Mark 13:13

Responsibilities

Somehow, gradually, you've been getting the message that it's time to step it up. Grades matter, you have more chores, and you might be learning new things (like how to drive). There may also be pressure to add new activities to your busy life – get a job, volunteer, join a club. The stress is enough to make you want to escape into your favorite show or video game. Creating margins of time in your schedule will be a life-long battle, so begin now to create good habits and even learn how to say 'no.'

My dilemma

_____
_____
_____
_____
_____
_____

Ideal outcome

_____
_____
_____
_____
_____

God's truth

Ecclesiastes 5:18-20 _____
1 Corinthians 9:24-27 _____
Galatians 6:9 _____
Colossians 3:23-24 _____
James 1:12 _____

How these truths apply to my situation

_____
_____
_____
_____
_____
_____

My convictions

_____
_____
_____
_____

My decisions

What am I feeling right now?
_____
_____

List all your responsibilities, and if they are optional (you can choose to give it up) or mandatory (you're stuck with it):
_____
_____
_____
_____
_____
_____

Mark with an asterisk on your list above any responsibilities that are temporary, and will end in the next 12 months.

Who do I think I would be disappointing if I let go of something on the list?
_____
_____
_____

Could a resolution be found in either getting out of any of the responsibilities, or persevering through them all? Why?
_____
_____
_____

What could be some positive things that can come from this struggle?
_____
_____
_____

Responsibilities

My decisions (continued)

Talk to God about it; write out what you want to do, what you are saying to God, what He is saying to you, and what events are unfolding, as you work at achieving your ideal outcome.

_____
_____
_____
_____
_____
_____
_____
_____

Final outcome

_____
_____
_____
_____
_____
_____
_____

You're in good company

Moses — read Exodus 3:1-11; 4:1,8-18

Esther — read Esther 1-9

Gideon — read Judges 6-7

I can do all of this through him who gives me strength.
— Philippians 4:13

Sibling Strife

The struggles with your siblings can come in many forms. Younger siblings might not respect your stuff or stay out of your room. Or maybe you have older siblings who don't treat you very nicely or who are so close to perfect that you feel like you live in their shadow. Tension can arise when there is jealousy, unhealthy competition, or disrespect. But you can be the one who returns your family dynamics back to God's design for it. Don't give up trying!

My dilemma

_____
_____
_____
_____
_____
_____

Ideal outcome

_____
_____
_____

God's truth

Psalm 69:8 (NLT) _____
James 1:19-21 _____
1 Peter 3:9 _____
Galatians 5:15 _____
Provers 19:11 _____
2 Timothy 2:23-24 _____

How these truths apply to my situation

_____
_____
_____
_____
_____

My convictions

_____
_____
_____
_____

My decisions

What am I feeling right now?
_____
_____

What's the worst thing that could happen if I tried to resolve this? Or if I don't?
_____
_____
_____

If I can't resolve it and it feels like I just have to cope, what is my prayer right now?
_____
_____
_____

What do I fear the most in this situation?
_____
_____
_____

What could be some positive things that can come from this struggle?
_____
_____
_____

What would it take to achieve my ideal outcome?
_____
_____
_____
_____

My decisions (continued)

Talk to God about it; write out what you want to do, what you are saying to God, what He is saying to you, and what events are unfolding, as you work at achieving your ideal outcome.

Final outcome

You're in good company

Jesus – read John 7:2-5
Joseph – read Genesis 37; 50:15-21
Caan & Abel – read Genesis 4:1-10
Jacob & Esau – Genesis 25:19-34; 27:1-45; 32:6-23; 33:1-11
Absalom/Amnon/Tamar/Solomon – read 2 Samuel 13

Let us therefore make every effort to do what leads to peace...
– Romans 14:19

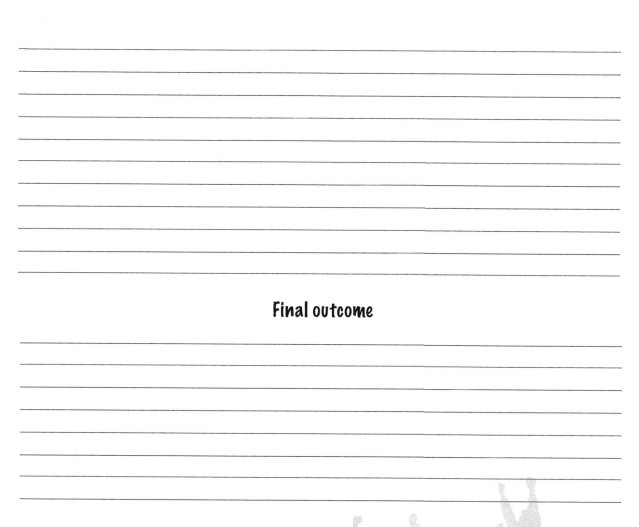

Sleep Deprived

Ever find yourself nodding off in class or have a difficult time concentrating while studying? Is it hard to get out of bed in the mornings? There are so many influences that affect your sleep during these growing years. Plus your body just needs more zzz's. It's biological! So it's up to you to create some good habits and stick to them. Your health, relationships, grades, commitments, and happiness all depend on it.

My dilemma

_____
_____
_____
_____
_____

Ideal outcome

_____
_____
_____
_____
_____

God's truth

Psalm 127:2 _____
Exodus 20:8-11 _____
Matthew 11:28-30 _____
Ecclesiastes 5:12 _____
Isaiah 40:28-31 _____
Psalm 3:5 _____

How these truths apply to my situation

_____
_____
_____
_____
_____

My convictions

_____
_____
_____
_____

My decisions

What am I feeling right now?
_____
_____

What's the worst thing that could happen if I tried to resolve this? Or if I don't?
_____
_____
_____

If I can't resolve it and it feels like I just have to cope, what is my prayer right now?
_____
_____
_____

What good habits can I begin making now to get more sleep?
_____
_____
_____

What activities or responsibilities might I need to give up in order to reclaim consistent sleep?
_____
_____
_____

What would it take to achieve my ideal outcome?
_____
_____
_____
_____

My decisions (continued)

Talk to God about it; write out what you want to do, what you are saying to God, what He is saying to you, and what events are unfolding, as you work at achieving your ideal outcome.

_____
_____
_____
_____
_____
_____
_____
_____
_____

Final outcome

_____
_____
_____
_____
_____
_____

You're in good company

Jesus – read Mark 6:30-34

Jacob – read Genesis 31:38-41

Paul – read 2 Corinthians 7:5; 11:24-27

You can go to bed without fear; you will lie down and sleep soundly.
– Proverbs 3:24 (NLT)

Temptation

The spiritual battle for your soul has been raging since the day you were born. Your sin nature, the alluring things of the world, and Satan's schemes are all working against you to pull you away from the fulfilling life that God has for you. Temptation landmines are EVERYWHERE. Begin by identifying what tempts you, then develop some healthy boundaries, and be willing to repent and ask God to help you start over (and over and over). The Holy Spirit in you will give you power to conquer them!

My dilemma

_____
_____
_____
_____

Ideal outcome

_____
_____
_____
_____

God's truth

1 Peter 5:8 _____
1 Corinthians 10:11-13 _____
James 1:13-15 _____
Matthew 26:41 _____
Psalm 119:9,11 _____
Hebrews 4:15 _____
James 4:7-8a _____
Galatians 5:16-24 _____

How these truths apply to my situation

_____
_____
_____
_____

My convictions

_____
_____
_____
_____

My decisions

What am I feeling right now?
_____
_____

What's the worst thing that could happen if I don't try to resolve this?
_____
_____
_____

If I can't resolve it and it feels like I just have to cope, what is my prayer right now?
_____
_____
_____

What boundaries do I need to set to be able to resist this temptation?
_____
_____
_____
_____

Who is someone I trust that I can share this with, for support and encouragement?
_____
_____
_____

What would it take to achieve my ideal outcome?
_____
_____
_____
_____
_____

My decisions (continued)

Talk to God about it; write out what you want to do, what you are saying to God, what He is saying to you, and what events are unfolding, as you work at achieving your ideal outcome.

Final outcome

You're in good company

Jesus – read Luke 4:1-13 and Hebrews 2:18; 4:15

Eve – read Genesis 3

David – read 2 Samuel 11

Because he himself suffered when he was tempted, he is able to help those who are being tempted.
— Hebrews 2:18

Uncontrollable Circumstances

All the hard work and good decisions you make in life won't protect you from experiencing circumstances that are out of your control. You might have been assigned a teacher you don't like, or your coach isn't giving you much playing time. Your best friend moved away, or mean kids just moved in next door. Life isn't fair. But thank goodness you can control some important things, like your attitude and your resolve to overcome.

My dilemma

_____
_____
_____
_____
_____

Ideal outcome

_____
_____
_____
_____
_____

God's truth

Ecclesiastes 9:11-12 _____
1 Kings 8:37 _____
2 Corinthians 1:9-10 _____
Philippians 4:12-13 _____
Exodus 14:13-14 _____
Isaiah 41:10,13 _____

How these truths apply to my situation

_____
_____
_____
_____
_____

My convictions

_____
_____
_____
_____

My decisions

What am I feeling right now?
_____
_____

What's the worst thing that could happen if I tried to resolve this? Or if I don't?
_____
_____
_____

If I can't resolve it and it feels like I just have to cope, what is my prayer right now?
_____
_____
_____

Is a positive outcome most likely found in getting out of the situation or persevering through it? Why?
_____
_____
_____
_____

What are some things I can control related to this struggle?
_____
_____
_____

What would it take to achieve my ideal outcome?
_____
_____
_____
_____

Uncontrollable Circumstances

My decisions (continued)

Talk to God about it; write out what you want to do, what you are saying to God, what He is saying to you, and what events are unfolding, as you work at achieving your ideal outcome.

Final outcome

You're in good company

Joseph – read Genesis 39:1-21; 40:1-23; 41:1-57

Shadrach/Meshach/Abednego – read Daniel 1:1-7; 3:1-30

Paul – read Acts 27:1-44 and Philippians 4:10-13 and 2 Corinthians 11:23-28,32-33

If we are thrown into the blazing furnace, the God we serve is able to deliver us from it...
– Daniel 3:17

Unknown Future

It has been relatively easy up until now to follow the path you have been on – most major decisions have been made for you. But now as a teenager your choices lead to achievements which lead to opportunities which lead to… adulthood. If you think the idea of the future is exhilarating, that is wonderful. You are about to embark on a thrilling new journey! If, however, it seems overwhelming, then remember that you are going through the necessary transition of becoming your own responsible young adult. God knows exactly where He's taking you. He'll give you your dreams, so you just follow His voice and He'll make those dreams come true.

My dilemma

_____
_____
_____
_____

Ideal outcome

_____
_____
_____
_____

God's truth

Deuteronomy 31:8 _____
Psalm 20:4 _____
Psalm 27:14 _____
Proverbs 3:5-6 _____
Proverbs 16:3,9 _____
Matthew 6:34 _____

How these truths apply to my situation

_____
_____
_____
_____

My convictions

_____
_____
_____
_____

My decisions

What am I feeling right now?
_____
_____

What's the worst thing that could happen if I tried to resolve this? Or if I don't?
_____
_____
_____

If I can't resolve it and it feels like I just have to cope, what is my prayer right now?
_____
_____
_____

Is a positive outcome most likely found in getting out of the situation or persevering through it? Why?
_____
_____
_____

How can I change my outlook on my future? Does this depend on me to do something?
_____
_____
_____

What would it take to achieve my ideal outcome?
_____
_____
_____
_____

Unknown Future

My decisions (continued)

Talk to God about it; write out what you want to do, what you are saying to God, what He is saying to you, and what events are unfolding, as you work at achieving your ideal outcome.

_____
_____
_____
_____
_____
_____
_____
_____
_____

Final outcome

_____
_____
_____
_____
_____
_____
_____

You're in good company

Joshua – read Deuteronomy 31:1-8 and Joshua 1:1-9

Mary – read Luke 1:26-38

Disciples – read John 16 and Acts 1:1-11

"For I know the plans I have for you," declares the Lord, "plans to prosper you and not to harm you, plans to give you hope and a future."

– Jeremiah 29:11

Note: Use these pages for another trial you are going through that isn't included.

My dilemma

Ideal outcome

God's truth

How these truths apply to my situation

My convictions

_____
_____
_____
_____

My decisions

What am I feeling right now?
_____
_____

What's the worst thing that could happen if I tried to resolve this? Or if I don't?
_____
_____
_____

If I can't resolve it and it feels like I just have to cope, what is my prayer right now?
_____
_____
_____

Is a positive outcome most likely found in getting out of the situation or persevering through it? Why?
_____
_____
_____
_____

How can I grow as a person from this struggle?
_____
_____
_____

What would it take to achieve my ideal outcome?
_____
_____
_____
_____
_____

My decisions (continued)

Talk to God about it; write out what you want to do, what you are saying to God, what He is saying to you, and what events are unfolding.

Final outcome

You're in good company

Who in the Bible has gone through this trial?

_____

_____

_____

Write out an encouraging verse or prayer:

Answered Prayers

Answered Prayers

Draw it Out

Draw it Out

Additional Scriptures

Addiction
Psalm 32:9 (NLT)
Psalm 69:5
Psalm 86:11
Psalm 119:133
Proverbs 21:25-26
Isaiah 57:15,18
John 10:10
Romans 7:21-8:9
Romans 12:1-2
Galatians 5:13,24
Galatians 6:7-8
Ephesians 2:3
Ephesians 4:17-19
Ephesians 6:10-13
Titus 1:7-8
Hebrews 10:26
James 4:4-8
2 Peter 1:5-9
1 John 3:3-9

Anxiety and Depression
Deuteronomy 31:8
Job 16:19-21
Psalm 73:21-26
Psalm 107:10,13-16
Psalm 139:23-24
John 16:33
Romans 8:6
Galatians 5:22-23
Philippians 4:6-9
Colossians 3:15
2 Thessalonians 3:16

Dating Dilemmas
Proverbs 13:20
Ephesians 4:1-3
1 Timothy 4:12

Failures
Psalm 86:6-7
Psalm 91:14-16
Psalm 119:50
Psalm 145:14
Proverbs 16:3-4a

Friendship Frustrations
Psalm 41:9
Psalm 109:1-5
Proverbs 12:26
Proverbs 18:24
Proverbs 27:6,9
1 Thessalonians 5:11

Health Concerns
Proverbs 3:7-8
Jeremiah 17:14
Jeremiah 30:17
Matthew 11:28-30
Romans 5:3-5
Romans 8:18

Loneliness
Psalm 23
Joshua 1:9

Additional Scriptures

Loss and Grief
Psalm 116:1-6
Psalm 147:3
2 Corinthians 1:3-4
James 5:10-11

Mean Messages
Psalm 25:19
Psalm 69:6-20
Psalm 89:50-51
Psalm 91:14-16
Proverbs 16:27 (NLT)
2 Corinthians 1:5-7
Hebrews 12:3

Money Matters
Deuteronomy 8:18
Psalm 112:5
Psalm 113:7
Proverbs 3:9-10
Proverbs 10:22
Proverbs 21:25-26
Matthew 6:25-34

Problems with Parents
Genesis 25:27-28
Leviticus 19:3
Proverbs 1:8-9
Proverbs 3:11-12

Rejection
Psalm 41:9
Romans 11:13-15

Responsibilities
Numbers 4:27
1 Corinthians 9:24-27
Galatians 6:2

Sibling Strife
Proverbs 18:19
Romans 12:17-19
1 Thessalonians 5:15
1 John 3:15

Sleep Deprivation
Genesis 2:3
Proverbs 10:5 (NLT)

Temptation
Galatians 5:13
Ephesians 6:10-13
Philippians 4:8

Uncontrollable Circumstances
Psalm 54
Psalm 107:23-30
Psalm 112:6-7

Unknown Future
Psalm 91:9-12
Psalm 107:4-9
Psalm 119:105
Psalm 121
Psalm 143:8
Isaiah 48:17

Dear reader,

I hope your *Teen Trials* journal has been a valuable resource in your faith journey! It is my prayer that you have learned how to find help from God in His word, as well as realize that many of your trials are not life-shattering but instead are opportunities for you to grow in character, maturity and faith.

*

If you are enjoying this journal, please…
- ☑ tell a friend about it!
- ☑ leave a review on Amazon
- ☑ tag me in a post with you and your journal

*

I would love to hear about your experience with this journal. You can connect with me here:

- ☑ *Instagram* @kimleaneauthor
- ☑ *Facebook* @kimleaneauthor
- ☑ *website* www.kimleane.com
- ☑ *email* contact@kimleane.com

*

Also, I invite you to join my VIP email list! The sign up form is right on my website. You can hear about my upcoming resources available for you, new discounts and promotions, and give me feedback when I need help writing. Plus you get a free gift for joining!

*

You have the strength and courage in you to turn your trials into triumphs, and when you don't feel like you have either, you have a Savior and King who will fight on your behalf! Remember, when you feel weak, Jesus loves to show off His strength in your life!

You are loved! *Kim*

About the Author

Kim is a wife and mom to 3 great kids — two teenagers and one tween. During a season in a spiritual desert while waiting on God to reveal what her "purpose" should be, Kim discovered that her purpose has always been the same, and what she should really be seeking is her next Kingdom Assignment. Through journaling, she saw how God was preparing her to create resources that help other believers on their discipleship journey, and spur them on to turn their faith into action.

Other Resources

A Disciple's Journal: Bearing Fruit is a full-color journal designed to help you dive deeper into the abundant life of fruitfulness as a follower of Jesus. It includes sections for:

- Writing down your "dialogue, downloads, and decisions with God"
- Encouraging the practice of spiritual disciplines
- Going deeper into discipleship through focused reflection questions, and
- Summarizing the highlights of your spiritual journey.

Check it out online at: bit.ly/bearingfruitjournal

Made in the USA
Coppell, TX
06 March 2020